THIS BOOK BELONGS TO:

NAME :

PHONE :

EMAIL :

Made in the USA
Monee, IL
05 November 2024

69383987R00070